GALE
CENGAGE Learning

Novels for Students, Volume 38

Project Editor: Sara Constantakis **Rights Acquisition and Management**: Margaret Chamberlain-Gaston, Tracie Richardson

Composition: Evi Abou-El-Seoud

Manufacturing: Rhonda Dover

Imaging: John Watkins

Product Design: Pamela A. E. Galbreath, Jennifer Wahi **Content Conversion**: Katrina Coach **Product Manager**: Meggin Condino

ISBN-10: 1-4144-6701-X
ISSN 1094-3552

This title is also available as an e-book.
ISBN-13: 978-1-4144-7367-3
ISBN-10: 1-4144-7367-2
Contact your Gale, a part of Cengage Learning sales
representative for ordering information.

Printed in Mexico
1 2 3 4 5 6 7 16 15 14 13 12

My Name Is Asher Lev

Chaim Potok 1972

Introduction

Chaim Potok's *My Name Is Asher Lev* was first published in 1972. The novel concerns the title character, a gifted young artist whose passion for drawing and painting is at odds with his strict Orthodox Jewish upbringing in the enclave of Crown Heights, Brooklyn, New York, during the 1950s and 1960s. As a somewhat autobiographical coming-of-age story, or bildungsro-man, the novel pits young Asher against his father, a highly respected member of the Ladover community who has devoted his life to establishing yeshivas (Jewish schools) in the United States and across Europe in the aftermath of World War II. Caught in the middle is Asher's mother, an emotionally fragile but well-educated woman who is torn between her love for her husband and her love for her son. Asher commits himself to the study of art and becomes the protégé and surrogate son of the great Jewish painter Jacob Kahn. The novel culminates in Asher's triumphant success in the New York art world with the unveiling of his twin masterpieces, *The Brooklyn Crucifixion I* and *The Brooklyn Crucifixion II*, paintings of his mother in a Christ-like pose, which prove to be the final straw that results in him being cast out of the Ladover community. The novel was a critical and commercial success, and it secured Potok's reputation as an American writer who portrays the cultural nuances of a very thin slice of society, the Hasidim, to the general reading public. He published a sequel, *The Gift of Asher Lev*, in 1990, in which Lev, now married and with a family, returns to Brooklyn after having lived abroad for many years.

Author Biography

Potok was born Herman Harold Potok on February 17, 1929, in the Bronx, New York, to Benjamin and Mollie Potok, both recent Polish immigrants and Orthodox Jews. As a boy, he enjoyed painting, but he decided at age sixteen to become a writer because it conflicted less with the family's religious beliefs. He remained equally committed to his religious studies and graduated at the top of his class from New York's Yeshiva University in 1950. Four years later, he graduated from the Jewish Theological Seminary and became a Conservative rabbi, which allowed him more freedom to pursue the arts than his former Orthodox affiliation did. Potok served as a chaplain during the Korean War, and in 1965, he received his Ph.D. in philosophy from the University of Pennsylvania. He legally changed his first name to Chaim (pronounced "*Hay*-yim") as an adult.

Inspired initially by Evelyn Waugh's *Brideshead Revisited* and James Joyce's *A Portrait of the Artist as a Young Man*, Potok loved literature, which displeased his parents, who expected him to become a doctor. Just like the fictional Asher Lev, Potok found his family and teachers dismissive of his desire to write because it was considered a frivolous occupation that would interfere with his studies of the Talmud, an important Jewish religious and philosophical text. This first-hand knowledge of the conflict between the religious and the secular is at the heart of *My Name Is Asher Lev*.

Potok published his first novel, *The Chosen*, to critical acclaim in 1967, and it was nominated for the National Book Award. The story concerns Danny Saunders's thirst for secular knowledge, which pits him against his father, a Hasidic rabbi, who expects his son to become a tzaddik, or spiritual leader, within their Orthodox community. Toward that end, his relationship with Danny is based solely on religion and lacks any personal connection beyond religion. Potok published a sequel, *The Promise*, in 1969, and followed it three years later with *My Name Is Asher Lev*.

Potok's subsequent novels, including *Davita's Harp* (1985) and *I Am the Clay* (1992), further cemented his reputation as his generation's foremost author concerned with the intersection of Judaism and American culture in the twentieth century. Apart from his fiction, Potok also published numerous nonfiction works on Jewish history, as well as short stories and essays for many literary journals. He wrote the critically acclaimed biography *My First 79 Years: Isaac Stern*, with the world-renowned violinist. *The Gift of Asher Lev* (1990) won the Jewish National Book Award in 1991, and his short story "Moon" won the O. Henry Award in 1999.

Potok married Adena Sarah Mosevitzky in 1958, and the couple had three children: Rena, Naama, and Akiva. Potok died of brain cancer on July 23, 2002, in Merion, Pennsylvania.

Book 1

CHAPTER 1

Asher Lev introduces himself as the artist of the infamous *Brooklyn Crucifixion I* and *Brooklyn Crucifixion II*, which he admits are highly unusual paintings for an Orthodox Jew. He recounts a bit of his family's history as Ladover Jews, a sect that stretches back several hundred years to feudal Russia. Asher was born to Rivkeh and Aryeh Lev in Crown Heights, Brooklyn, in 1943. His father works for the Rebbe, the Ladover leader, traveling throughout the country helping Jews emigrate from the Stalinist Soviet Union and settle in the United States.

The events of the story begin when Asher is six. He is a precocious artist who enjoys drawing realistic portraits, especially of his mother. Riv-keh encourages him to draw "pretty" pictures, but Aryeh hopes the boy will outgrow what he believes is a useless hobby. Asher's Uncle Yitzchok, a watchmaker and diamond merchant, encourages the boy's art and introduces him to the works of Pablo Picasso and the Jewish painter Marc Chagall. Asher meets Reb Yudel Krinsky, one of the few Russian Ladovers to make it safely to the United States after being imprisoned for many years in the Gulag, a network of Siberian work camps, where his wife and children, imprisoned along with him, have died. He works at a stationary shop where Asher buys his paper and pencils.

Rivkeh's beloved older brother, Asher's Uncle Yaakov, dies in a car accident while traveling on behalf of the Rebbe, sending Rivkeh into a deep clinical depression that requires hospitalization and many months of convalescence, during which she is so consumed with grief that she cannot take care of her young son. During this time, Aryeh stays home to take care of Asher. When Rivkeh recovers, she wants to continue her brother's work by becoming a professor of Russian studies. In a highly unusual move, the Rebbe agrees that this would be the best use of her talents. Rivkeh begins college at the same time Asher begins his formal education at yeshiva.

CHAPTER 2

Asher abandons art for several years, and Aryeh resumes traveling for the Rebbe. When he is out of town, Rivkeh is beside herself with worry, fearing that he will die just like her brother. Slowly the Brooklyn Ladover community grows as more Jews arrive from Europe and the Soviet Union. Joseph Stalin continues to persecute Jews, killing many of them or sending them to the Gulag. Two highly publicized cases involve a group of Jewish writers and a group of Jewish doctors, both convicted and sentenced to death on trumped-up charges of crimes against the state. Asher learns that Reb Yudel Krinsky was apprehended by the Stalinist regime, even though no one in his community objected to the presence of the Ladovers.

Asher is a poor student. His father is dismayed at his lack of discipline with schoolwork. It is expected that, because he is the son of one of the Rebbe's most valuable advisors, he will follow in Aryeh's footsteps as a Talmudic scholar.

CHAPTER 3

Stalin dies, and the Ladover community is relieved. The Rebbe decides that Aryeh must move to Vienna to establish yeshivas throughout the major cities of Europe. Asher, who has taken up drawing again with a vengeance, stubbornly objects to moving. His relationship with his father has become strained because of his artistic obsession and corresponding lack of interest in school, and he cannot bear to contemplate life beyond his comfortable Crown Heights neighborhood. He does not want to fly on an airplane, learn a new language, or make new friends. He pesters his parents incessantly not to go. The Rebbe insists that Aryeh go, but Rivkeh, although she supports her husband, wants to stay to finish her education and be a good mother to Asher.

Media Adaptations

- Aaron Posner adapted and directed *My Name Is Asher Lev* as a stage play, which premiered at the Arden Theatre in Philadelphia in 2009. Potok's widow, Adena Potok, served as an artistic consultant for the production. Posner had previously worked with Chaim Potok on a stage adaptation of *The Chosen* in 2000.

CHAPTER 4

Asher is now ten years old. His gift for art has become a powerful presence in his life and influences how he perceives the world. He draws unconsciously and compulsively. At school, he unthinkingly draws a picture of Joseph Stalin in his coffin. Aryeh is very angry that the boy draws when he should be studying. He begins to think that Asher's gift may come from the *sitra achra*, the Other Side, the source of evil. Asher has ominous dreams about his mythic ancestor, a black-garbed man who represents his guilt over his unwillingness to be a dutiful son.

CHAPTER 5

Asher's artistic inclination reaches a crisis point. He unthinkingly defiles his Chumash (a bound copy of the Torah) by drawing a picture of the Rebbe in it. This convinces his teacher that his gift is from the Other Side. Asher's classmates as well as his mashpia (headmaster) taunt him. At home, father and son continually clash over art. Aryeh rebukes him for being disrespectful and forbids him to draw any more.

The Rebbe invites Asher to draw several pictures for him. Afterward, Asher goes to a museum instead of returning home. He is gone so long his mother calls the police. The next day, Asher steals oil paints from Krinsky's store but is too guilt-ridden to use them.

Miraculously to Asher, the Rebbe has decided that Asher is truly gifted and does not have to move to Vienna. Thus, Aryeh leaves for Vienna, while Rivkeh and Asher stay behind.

Book 2

CHAPTER 6

Rivkeh is now in graduate school and misses Aryeh terribly. Her separation anxiety is the result of having lost her parents at a young age, after which she and her brother lived with their aunt until she also died. Now, Rivkeh has lost her brother and fears that Aryeh is next. Asher also misses his father and starts drawing pictures of him, wondering whether he and his mother should move to Vienna to be with him after all.

On December 26, 1953, Rivkeh presents Asher with his first set of oil paints. He becomes obsessed with painting immediately and neglects studying the Torah, which is essential to his upcoming bar mitzvah. Adding to the scandal is the fact that Asher's father is risking his life to bring the Torah to people in Europe while his own son is ignoring it. Mrs. Rackover, his baby-sitter, refuses to speak to him.

At the Parkway Museum, Asher is exposed to Christian and Western iconography, including crucifixions and nudes. Rivkeh tells him that such art is inappropriate and reminds him that Jews do not paint. Furthermore, she is afraid the museum will lead him away from his Orthodox heritage and toward Christianity. When Asher begins drawing pictures of Jesus and nudes, she is horrified. Asher's mind, however, is only on art; his religious belief never wavers. He misses his father on Shabbos (Sabbath) and during the Jewish holidays, and apart from his lack of interest in school, he remains pious.

When Aryeh returns to Brooklyn for a visit, he is physically gaunt and enraged over Asher's use of

Jesus as a subject of his paintings. He is angry with Rivkeh for encouraging him, but she explains that she provided Asher with art supplies because she thought it would prompt him to study harder. Discord reigns; Asher's father demands he stop drawing, grabs his wrist to keep him from tracing shapes on the table with his fork, and compares him to an animal that has no control over its actions. His will to draw is evil, in Aryeh's eyes, and he believes Asher should never have been born.

Rivkeh is torn; she agrees with her husband yet still loves her son. Rivkeh's torment reaches excruciating levels when Aryeh is sent to Russia and no one hears from him for months. The following summer, Rivkeh, now working on her Ph.D., sails to Vienna to be with Aryeh, and Asher stays with his Uncle Yitzchok. Reb Krinsky gets married.

CHAPTER 7

Following Asher's bar mitzvah, the Rebbe arranges for him to study with Jacob Kahn, a famous artist who is a non-observant Jew. At their first meeting, Jacob tells Asher he would be better off becoming a street cleaner. Becoming an artist will cause trouble and heartache for him given his Ladover heritage. Asher is surprised to see that Jacob has drawings he made years ago for the Rebbe.

Chapter 8

Jacob begins Asher's education by having him

study Picasso's *Guernica* at the Museum of Modern Art. Throughout the winter, Asher does just that, and he returns to Jacob's studio in the spring to start his apprenticeship. This entails studying the New Testament of the Bible so the boy can understand many of Western art's greatest works. He also studies paintings by the Jewish artists Modigliani, Soutine, and Pascin. Asher's apprenticeship is to last five years.

Asher meets Anna Schaeffer, Jacob's art dealer, who calls Jacob "a mean, tricky, and nasty old man" for not telling her that his protégé is a thirteen-year-old Orthodox Jewish boy. She becomes Asher's closest link to the secular world and is focused on making money. As a gallery owner and art dealer, she is good at what she does.

At home, Rivkeh is worried sick about Aryeh —he was supposed to come home for Pesach (Passover), but no one knows where he is.

CHAPTER 9

Aryeh turns up in Vienna after Passover. Rivkeh can bear his absence no longer and travels to Vienna to be with him. Asher moves into his Uncle Yitzchok's house and scandalizes the family by painting without his shirt on. Jacob hires a model for Asher to paint nude, and Asher is tormented because he promised the Rebbe he would never do such a thing. Jacob assures him that it is not a sin to paint a beautiful girl. Asher relents but finds the process difficult, and he grows into it slowly.

While his parents come home to visit for a

month and a half, Asher does not see Jacob. Aryeh looks haggard and is still not reconciled to the path the Rebbe has chosen for Asher. Rivkeh has finished her dissertation and wants to move to Vienna with her husband permanently. Asher objects; he doesn't mind staying with his uncle for a little while, but he cannot bear the thought of living there permanently. Rivkeh tells Asher he is selfish and acting childish. Asher dreams again of his mythic ancestor.

When Asher falls asleep in class one day, his teacher calls him Rembrandt Lev; the Rebbe cautions the boy against entering the Other Side. Asher dislikes living with his uncle because he is fat, rich, and boorish.

CHAPTER 10

Jacob and his wife Tanya invite Asher to spend the summer with them in Provincetown, Massachusetts, an artists' enclave on Cape Cod. When Asher tucks his long earlocks (hair dangling in front of the ears, worn in compliance with tradition) behind his ears, Jacob cautions Asher to be true to himself and not to be ashamed of his Ladover roots. Asher remains kosher and observant to the point that he does not paint on Shabbos. Tanya warns Asher that the world is not nice to good people like him.

CHAPTER 11

Uncle Yitzchok fixes up the attic as a studio for Asher, and Jacob's latest show at Anna's gallery sells out. Jacob and Asher travel to various museums in the country to study art. Asher's parents come back to Brooklyn for a visit and Aryeh looks much better now that he has Rivkeh to care for him. However, a permanent rift has developed between Asher and his father, and when Rivkeh urges Asher to come to Europe, he declines.

After another summer in Provincetown, Asher decides it is time to visit Europe. He becomes violently ill on the plane ride over and remains bedridden during his short stay. He returns home to Provincetown with Jacob and Tanya.

That fall, the Rebbe decides Asher will study Russian in college while he continues attending yeshiva. He refuses until the Rebbe explains that he expects Asher to become a great artist who will travel to Russia. Anna Schaeffer's first show of Asher's work is a moderate success that leaves them neither rich nor poor. His second show is more successful. Asher's parents do not come to either show because they feature paintings of nudes.

Aryeh's work in Europe is finally done, and he and Rivkeh move back into their old house in Crown Heights. Asher remains at his Uncle Yitzchok's.

CHAPTER 12

Aryeh's success has garnered him a revered place in the community, and Rivkeh is happy to have him safely at home now. Their time together in Europe has given them many experiences that make Asher feel left out, but at least Aryeh's rage at his son has dissipated into a tolerable lack of interest. While he is glad that his son's art is successful and that he has not shamed them, Aryeh is not interested in hearing about or seeing Asher's work.

Asher spends the summer with Jacob and Tanya in Provincetown instead of in the Berkshires with his parents. When Asher travels to museums throughout the country with Jacob, the Rebbe gives him messages to deliver to other Ladover Jews.

Eventually, Asher's career begins to eclipse that of Jacob, who is now eighty years old. He realizes that it's time for him to go to Europe in order for his inspiration to be renewed. Jacob tells him that Florence is a gift.

CHAPTER 13

In Florence, Asher is profoundly affected by Michelangelo's *Pieta*, a sculpture of Mary, mother of Jesus Christ, embracing Christ's dead body, and his David, a statue of the brave young king as he faces Goliath in battle. His reaction has nothing to do with their Christian subject matter and everything to do with their depiction of pain and suffering. He begins to sketch the *Pieta* and finds that Mary resembles his mother. The mythic ancestor returns in his dreams.

In Rome, Asher is met by a Ladover Jew who takes him to a yeshiva established by Asher's father. The man calls Aryeh Lev remarkable. In Paris, Asher meets another Ladover Jew, Avraham Cutler, the son of his old mashpia, or mentor, who invites him to stay at the yeshiva established by his father.

Asher rents a studio in Paris and begins painting, eating his meals at the yeshiva. Anna Schaeffer is excited by Asher's new direction. He begins to paint his mythic ancestor, and he is obsessed by his mother's suffering over the loss of her brother, her fear for Aryeh's safety, and the strain he has placed on her. The result is two paintings: *The Brooklyn Crucifixion I* and *The Brooklyn Crucifixion II*. The former portrays Rivkeh framed against the slatted window shades of their Crown Heights living room in a vaguely Christ-like way. The latter renders her in a much more intentional crucifixion pose, her face split into three angles as Aryeh and Asher look upon her.

Anna Schaeffer comes to visit, and she is awestruck by the paintings. She ships them out of the country without obtaining Asher's permission, confident they are masterpieces. She begins to plan a show that she is sure will cement his reputation in the art world.

CHAPTER 14

Asher arrives unannounced in New York for his show and everyone is happy to see him. Anna announces that most of the paintings have sold even before the show has opened, including both of the *Brooklyn Crucifixions*. Asher is worried; he knows the paintings will hurt people, but Anna dispassionately reminds him that great art hurts people. He returns to his childhood home to find his mother waiting in the window for him, just as in his painting. Both Rivkeh and Aryeh have decided to come to his opening because none of the paintings feature nudes. However, Asher does not tell them about the Crucifixions.

Aryeh's reaction to the works is "awe and rage and bewilderment and sadness, all at the same time."; He leaves abruptly, stating that Asher has exceeded "limits." He and Rivkeh no longer want anything to do with him.

In a final meeting with the Rebbe, Asher is told that his gift has caused harm. "You are alone now," he says, and asks Asher to leave the Ladover community.

Rav Avraham Cutler

Avraham Cutler ("Rav" is a title meaning Rabbi) is the son of Rav Josef Cutler, Asher's yeshiva mashpia (mentor or spiritual leader), and he is the mashpia of the yeshiva in Paris established by Aryeh Lev. He tells Asher that his father and the Rebbe are great, wise men, and he invites Asher to stay in Paris and welcomes him to eat his meals at the yeshiva. Asher finds him friendly and accommodating.

Rav Josef Cutler

Josef Cutler is the mashpia of Asher's yeshiva and the father of Avraham Cutler. Although he is often dismissive of Asher's artwork, he brings the boy's talent to the Rebbe's attention.

Jacob Kahn

Jacob Kahn is a famous and successful painter who is in his early seventies when Asher meets him. The Rebbe has handpicked Jacob to be Asher's mentor, even though the artist is no longer an observant Jew. Jacob respects Asher's Orthodox ways and wants him to remain true to who he is in order for his art to have merit. Initially, however,

Jacob tells Asher to become a street cleaner, because being an artist will be tortuous and painful. Jacob once lived in Paris and painted with Pablo Picasso and other famous artists of the day.

Jacob takes his role as Asher's mentor seriously, exposing the boy to the traditions he must be familiar with and traveling with him to museums throughout the country. He has a love-hate relationship with his art dealer, Anna Schaeffer, who has made him wealthy and established his reputation. He wishes he could remain contemptuous of the commercial and promotional aspects of the art world, as Picasso does.

Jacob and his wife, Tanya, had no children, and they treat Asher like a son, hosting him for the summer in Provincetown, Massachusetts. Jacob is supportive of Asher's decision to travel to Europe and knows it will help him grow as an artist. When he is nearing eighty and in decline as Asher's reputation is on the rise, he becomes slightly bitter and jealous.

Tanya Kahn

Tanya Kahn is Jacob's wife. She is motherly toward Asher and welcomes him for the summer to their home in Provincetown.

Reb Yudel Krinsky

Reb Yudel Krinsky is a Russian Jew who has recently arrived in Brooklyn after spending several years exiled in Siberia, where his wife and children died in the Gulag work camps. He works at a stationery shop where Asher buys his art supplies. Krinsky encourages Asher's art, and in turn Asher becomes interested in the story of his life before he came to America. Later, Krinsky marries again and has two more children.

Aryeh Lev

Aryeh Lev is Asher's father and Rivkeh's husband. He is devout, highly educated, and highly respected in the community, but he is intolerant of his son's artistic ambition and supremely disappointed in Asher's lack of interest in schoolwork and Talmudic studies. He faithfully serves the Ladover Rebbe, doing what he is told for the sake of the community's survival and growth. His faithfulness and devotion help many families escape from repressive regimes in Europe after World War II. Later, he establishes many yeshivas in Europe; when Asher visits them, he finds that they are thriving. Aryeh is regarded by all who know him as a wise man.

Aryeh is lost without his wife, and when he returns from Vienna he is haggard and sickly. His stamina and health return when Rivkeh joins him permanently in Europe. His affection for her never wavers.

Despite his intelligence, Aryeh does not understand art and makes no attempt to do so in order to understand his son. He believes Asher's gift for art is from the evil Other Side and will lead to his son's abandonment of his Ladover religion. While Aryeh never approves of his son's choices and has previously forbidden him from drawing, he does not disown Asher completely until he sees the *Brooklyn Crucifixions*. The paintings are the final straw that severs their relationship forever because of their portrayal of Rivkeh using symbolism established by Christians, some of whom have persecuted and killed Jews for centuries.

Asher Lev

As the novel opens, Asher Lev is a successful young artist. His most famous works, the autobiographical *Brooklyn Crucifixions*, have brought him notoriety for using Christian symbols to convey the rift in his Orthodox Jewish family. Asher then recounts his life from the time he was six years old in the late 1940s. He was a precocious artist as a young boy, concerned more with conveying emotional truths in his drawing than creating "pretty pictures." His most frequent subject is his mother, Rivkeh. He is close to her and he feels her suffering acutely.

Asher is a solitary, serious boy who loves to draw and does not apply himself to his schoolwork. He is expected to follow in his father's footsteps and become a Talmudic scholar, but his lack of focus in school leaves his elders disappointed in him. When his father announces they are moving to Vienna, Asher adamantly refuses to go. He is petulant, stubborn, and selfish.

When it comes to their Orthodox sect, the Ladover, Asher never questions his faith, even when it conflicts with his quest to become an artist. He remains observant as long as religious traditions do not conflict with his art. When they do, he favors art, but he never abandons the beliefs and traditions of the Ladover Hasidim.

The stronger Asher's allegiance to art grows, the more others become convinced his gift comes from the sitra achra—the Other Side. He puts art ahead of God and family, in direct defiance of the commandments. He follows his own path, rather than the path that tradition dictates, and the guilt he feels is represented by his recurring dreams of his mythic ancestor.

Asher pushes boundaries to the extreme, but does not object when the Rebbe banishes him from the Crown Heights Ladover community.

Rivkeh Lev

Rivkeh Lev is Asher's mother and Aryeh's wife. For most of the novel, she is torn between her love for her husband and her son. Both need her, and yet their divergent paths mean she can please only one. Rivkeh's suffering is Asher's inspiration for the *Brooklyn Crucifixions*.

A turning point in her life is the death of her beloved brother, Yaakov, in a car accident while traveling on behalf of the Rebbe. She blames the

Rebbe for his death, and she suffers a mental breakdown that leaves her hospitalized and incapacitated for several months. Upon recovering, she decides to continue her brother's work by going to college and becoming a professor of Russian studies.

She doggedly pursues her studies but is forever worried about her husband, who continues traveling on behalf of the Rebbe. When he moves to Vienna and she remains in Brooklyn with Asher, her obsessive worrying intensifies.

Rivkeh is ambivalent about her son's decision to become an artist and dislikes the strain it puts on his relationship with Aryeh. She buys him art supplies, mainly so he will stop stealing from Krinsky but also in hopes that he will repay her by taking his studies more seriously.

Rivkeh understands Asher's obsession with art, because it is similar to her obsession with completing her brother's work. She is almost as much of an anomaly in their community as her son is. Both are pursuing nontraditional paths, so she supports him as much as she can, but ultimately her allegiance is with her husband and her religion. She views the *Brooklyn Crucifixions* as an unpardonable sin and the final betrayal of her love for him.

Uncle Yitzchok Lev

Yitzchok is Aryeh's brother. He is a watchmaker and diamond merchant who, according to Asher, is fat, wealthy, and boorish. He supports the young Asher's interest in art, introducing him to the art of Picasso and Chagall. When Rivkeh joins Aryeh in Europe, Asher stays with Yitzchok in his Crown Heights home. To support the boy, Yitzchok converts the large attic into a studio, but he is surprised and dismayed to find the boy painting in the summer heat without his shirt on. Although Yitzchok is more accepting of culture outside their Orthodox sect than Aryeh is, he, too, cautions Asher from going too far with his art.

Mythic Ancestor

Asher's mythic ancestor comes to him in dreams. In the time of the Black Death in Europe in 1347, this ancestor helped a drunken nobleman become wealthy. As a form of penance for the ruthless deeds of the nobleman, which included burning down a village and killing its residents, the mythic ancestor began traveling in order to bring the Master of the Universe to the world, a trend that continues with Asher's father. This good, wise, and selfless man haunts Asher's dreams as a shadowy, dark menace. He represents Asher's guilt over not following in his father's footsteps, knowing that he should respect the family's tradition of traveling and teaching. The mythic ancestor reproaches Asher for his art.

Mrs. Rackover

Mrs. Rackover is a neighbor and fellow Ladover Jew who watches young Asher after school when his parents are not around. She disproves of Asher's immersion in art and his bad habit of coming home late from school. She stops speaking to him after a while because of his impertinence. She dies in a car accident in Detroit—just as Asher's Uncle Yaakov did.

The Rebbe

The Rebbe is the spiritual leader of the Ladover community in Crown Heights. He is revered and trusted by all in the Orthodox sect and is believed to have spiritual wisdom that allows him to determine the course of each Ladover's life. Because the Rebbe has decided that Aryeh must move to Europe to build yeshivas, Aryeh unquestioningly does so. Rivkeh wants to continue her brother's work by becoming a scholar of Russian studies and is surprised when the Rebbe allows it, for such education for a woman is uncommon in the patriarchal community.

The Rebbe understands that Asher's gift cannot be ignored and realizes that Asher's path in life will not be that of his father's. Thus, he tries to keep Asher within the community by allowing him to apprentice with Jacob Kahn. He makes Jacob promise not to force the boy to paint nudes or participate in forbidden behaviors. Thus, the Rebbe proves himself a man of reason and compassion who understands people's strengths and weaknesses and tries to accommodate them for the good of the community.

The Rebbe banishes Asher at the end of the novel, telling him his paintings have exceeded the limits of what is acceptable to remain within the Crown Heights Ladover community. He has hurt people, and because of that he must leave. The Rebbe bears some resemblance to Rebbe Menachem Mendel Schneerson, who was the spiritual leader of the Brooklyn-based Luba-vitcher Hasidim in the 1950s and 1960s.

Anna Schaeffer

Anna Schaeffer is Jacob's art dealer, a single-minded woman in her sixties who loves money and considers Jacob a tricky old man. For Asher, she represents the secular world. At first, she is chagrined to find out that Jacob's protégéis an Orthodox Jewish boy, but she quickly recognizes his talent and is eager to promote his work in the New York art world, positive it will make them both very wealthy. She is unconcerned about the effect of Asher's art on those he loves. She is interested only in making his reputation, earning them both much money, and further establishing her preeminence in the art world.

She refuses to serve kosher food at her openings because she is in the business of catering not to Jews but to art patrons. She is elated when Asher decides to move to Paris to paint, believing that "Asher Lev in Paris" represents a turning point in his career that will transform him from a promising artist into a great artist. She sends him a beret for good measure, which he never wears. When she visits and lays eyes on the *Brooklyn Crucifixions*, she is awestruck. She hustles the paintings out of the country before Asher can object. Anna is good at her job; she knows a masterpiece when she sees one. She believes that great art hurts people and that Asher needs to come to terms with the fact.

Uncle Yaakov

Yaakov is Rivkeh's older brother. While traveling for the Rebbe in Detroit, he dies in a car accident. His death sends Rivkeh into a spiral of despair. They were particularly close because their parents had died when they were young, and Yaakov had looked after his sister like a father. He was supposed to become a professor of Russian studies at New York University.

Jewish Culture

My Name Is Asher Lev delves into the world of Orthodox Judaism in its portrayal of the close-knit Ladover community in Crown Heights, Brooklyn. The Ladover Jews are Orthodox, Hasidic Jews who believe that the Torah is the word of God. Their term for God is "Master of the Universe," and their spiritual leader is the Rebbe, a universally acknowledged wise man whose pronouncements are held as law by the sect's adherents. The clash between Asher Lev and his father, a highly respected member of the community, highlights the beliefs and customs of a religious group with which many non-Jewish readers may not be familiar. Beginning with the strong devotion to scholarly and religious studies and a suspicion of artistic pursuits, the culture of the Ladover, who resemble the real-life Lubavitcher Jews, is in direct conflict with Asher's desire to become an artist. Potok, as a Conservative rabbi, portrays the nuances of this clash between the quest for personal fulfillment and domestic harmony, which is the concept of *shalom bayit*. Aryeh and Rivkeh have devoted their lives to following the Rebbe's decisions, even though it has meant that they spend much time apart, which is very painful for Rivkeh.

Asher attends a yeshiva, a Jewish school,

where the young boy is chastised for desecrating his Chumash, a bound copy of the Torah, with a drawing. The pursuit of art is frivolous for the Ladover, who believe that such a secular talent could be from the sitra achra, the Other Side.

Potok describes the physical appearance of the Ladover, which is similar to most Orthodox Jews. Men wear black hats and full beards, and they wear their hair in earlocks, or payots, in accordance with the book of Leviticus. They wear prayer shawls with tzitzit, a form of tassel that keeps the commandments between their hands and their heart. Their modest appearance reflects their conservative beliefs. When Asher is caught painting in the summer heat with his shirt off, his Uncle Yitz-chok is scandalized. Orthodox men wear black suits and black hats; women wear hats or wigs.

As Orthodox Jews, the Ladover keep kosher, meaning their dietary habits are strict; this means that, when Asher travels abroad, he can eat only in certain establishments known to maintain kosher kitchens. They observe daily prayer rituals and take a ritual bath known as a mikvah. Passover and Shabbos (Sabbath) are strictly observed. Even in the summertime when Asher is on vacation with Jacob, he refrains from painting on Shabbos.

That Asher's gift might be from the sitra achra —the Other Side, meaning from a darkness devoid of the Master of the Universe—is an idea that is specifically Hasidic. Mainstream Christian art reveres the form of Jesus and has a long, illustrious history. Representations of biblical themes are considered inspirational and have been commissioned for centuries by popes and other church officials. The Jewish religion, however, takes seriously the commandment against creating graven images (literally, this means pictures that are carved or engraved, but it is extended to include all representational art). Thus, most Jewish art is relegated to the decorative arts and is thought to be trivial; greater importance is placed on scholarly study as the path to closeness to God.

Parent-Child Relationships

As a bildungsroman—a coming-of-age story —*My Name Is Asher Lev* necessarily concerns young Asher's relationship with his parents. It is a complicated relationship, infused with love and the frustration of parents who want what is best for their only child.

Topics for Further Study

- Write a bildungsroman (a coming-of-age story) that summarizes your life so far. Organize it around a conflict you have experienced. Include a symbol in the story that represents that conflict (similar to Asher's mythic ancestor) and choose an epigraph (a phrase, quotation, or poem that introduces the story) that relates to your experience.

- Create a slide show of works of Jewish art, set to Yiddish music. Include ten works of twentieth-century art from Jewish artists and ten works of the decorative arts created for use during Jewish holidays. The Jewish Museum (http://www.thejewishmuseum.org) is a good source for these. Pair the artworks with the holiday items in such a way that their similarities and differences are highlighted. Present the slide show to the class, explaining your reasoning for arranging each pair of works in a particular way.

- *Rosanna of the Amish* (1947, reprinted 2008) by Joseph Warren Yoder is a young-adult story about an Irish orphan who is adopted by a single Amish woman. The book, written by an Amish author, sympathetically explores the unique customs and traditions of America's Old Order Amish sects. Write a paper describing the similarities and differences between the Amish as portrayed by Yoder and the Lubavitcher Jews as portrayed by Potok. Apart from the obvious differences between Judaism and Christianity, discuss how each group's customs and rituals compare.

- Research the modern Jewish Diaspora and create a chart depicting the number of Jews who lived in Russia, Poland, Germany, France, Palestine, Great Britain, Canada, and the United States prior to World War II and how many live in those countries today. Create another chart illustrating the world's Jewish population just prior to World War II, immediately following World War II, and today. What do the charts tell you about immigration patterns?

- Using Microsoft Excel and referring to the tutorials found at http://www.microsoft.com/education/Cr(create a time line that includes both the events of My Name *Is Asher Lev* and the real-life events of the Holocaust, the Stalinist Soviet

Union, the formation of the state of Israel, and the creation of the Lubavitcher Hasidim and its move to New York. Also plot the creation of Michelangelo's *Pieta* and *David*, Picasso's Guernica, and the creation of key works by Marc Chagall. Include some historical events that relate to art and Jewish history as well.

Asher's relationship with Rivkeh and Aryeh is full of the push and pull of parents trying to shepherd their child into successful adulthood. Rivkeh, despite her fragile emotional health, clearly loves Asher and encourages his artistic talent while he is young. Because of her own desire to pursue a nontraditional path (for an Orthodox Jewish woman), she sympathizes with his love of art. When Asher refuses to move to Vienna, Rivkeh agrees to stay behind in Brooklyn to care for him.

Asher's relationship with his father is fraught with tension from the beginning. By the time Asher starts school, Aryeh expects him to abandon his childish pursuit of art. When he refuses, Aryeh admonishes the boy's poor performance, which reflects badly on his own reputation as a scholar and esteemed member of the Ladover community. As an Orthodox family, the Levs expect complete faithfulness from their son in accordance with their traditions. Aryeh can only think that Asher's unwillingness to obey and follow a predetermined path similar to his father's is evidence that his artistic talent is from the sitra achra, the realm of the unholy.

Asher does not willingly defy his parents; rather, he follows his heart, which leads him away from the family. He recognizes the terrible strain this puts on his parents, but he is unwilling to compromise. The result of the parent-child relationship is made manifest in Asher's unflinching family portrait *The Brooklyn Crucifixion II*, in which Rivkeh is shown suffering on a symbolic cross, torn between her husband and her son.

Creative Process

My Name Is Asher Lev documents a young artist's coming of age. Potok's depictions of Asher's creative process allow the reader to glimpse how he develops his gift and how the gift manifests as a mystical force that the boy cannot control. He draws in his sleep and during class, steals art supplies, and is ultimately beholden to his talent. When he is little more than a toddler, Asher uses cigarette ashes to shade a drawing of his unhappy mother. For Asher, art is never about an idealized world but rather about showing the world as it really is.

Part of the creative process entails learning about art. Asher escapes to the Parkway Museum, where he sees Christian iconography for the first time. Outside the enclosed world of the Hasidim, he sees nudes and paintings of the Virgin Mary, causing him to ask questions his parents would rather not hear.

Another part of the creative process is Asher's apprenticeship with Jacob Kahn, who tells him it would be better if he became a street cleaner. Jacob understands that remaining faithful to one's artistic vision will cause pain, both for the artist and for his loved ones. Anna Schaeffer, Asher's dealer, tells him the same thing.

For Asher, the creative process requires that he be true to himself, no matter how much trouble it causes, no matter what religious customs he betrays. He refuses to move to Vienna with his father, and he draws nudes in defiance of his religion's prohibition against it. To Aryeh, Asher's inability to control his gift is evidence of his animal nature, because people should be able to control themselves.

Asher follows his creative education to its bittersweet conclusion: he uses Western Christian symbolism in a painting involving his Orthodox mother. In the aftermath of the resulting scandal, Asher is cast out of the Brooklyn Ladover community. Rather than devoting his life to Talmudic study for the betterment of the community, he has devoted it to his own creative fulfillment. His gift is irrevocably at odds with his religious beliefs.

Bildungsroman/Kunstlerroman

A bildungsroman is a coming-of-age story that depicts the growth of a young protagonist into a psychologically mature adult. *My Name Is Asher Lev* is a bildungsroman in the sense that Asher is around six years old when the story begins and a young adult by the time it ends; the story's action concerns his psychological development as a young man at odds with his family and community. He is a stubborn teenager but a devoted protégé. Potok presents the boy's maturation process, including his drawing and painting techniques, his study of art history, the personal obstacles he overcomes, and the choices he makes on the costly road to success. Many bildungsromans are told in first person, because such a technique allows the author to convey the protagonist's thoughts as they mature from childhood to adulthood.

A kunstlerroman, literally an "artist's novel," is a specific type of bildungsroman that focuses on the maturation of an artist. *My Name Is Asher Lev* neatly falls into this category because its sole focus is the development of Asher from a precocious boy into a talented artist, a journey that results in his banishment from his tight-knit community. The novel is often compared to James Joyce's *A Portrait of the Artist as a Young Man*, which inspired Potok when he was beginning his writing career.

Symbolism

A symbol is an object that represents something other than itself. Judaism is full of symbols (as are most religions), such as the Hanukkah menorah in which each candle symbolizes one day of the eight-day festival. One of the most obvious symbols in *My Name Is Asher Lev* is Asher's mythic ancestor, the reproachful, dark-garbed man who comes to him in dreams. The mythic ancestor is a vision of a real-life forefather from feudal Russia who devoted himself to bringing the Master of the Universe through his travels and teaching. When he appears in Asher's dreams, the mythic ancestor represents Asher's guilt in not following his family's tradition of traveling and teaching on behalf of the Ladover.

Another major symbol in the novel is the crucifixion. In Christianity, the crucifixion refers to Jesus' death on the cross at the hands of the Romans. For centuries, depictions of the crucifixion have been a staple of Western art, reminding Christians of Jesus' suffering in return for their eternal salvation. Jews, however, do not believe that Jesus was the Messiah, and thus his death has no symbolic value in itself. However, when Asher first sees the crucifixions at the art museum, he sees in them a heart-rending expression of suffering in a human, but not religious, way. His *Brooklyn Crucifixions* depict his mother on a cross not in a religious sense but to convey her extreme suffering in the battle between her husband and her son and also the terror she experienced each time Aryeh traveled on behalf of the Rebbe.

However, for Rivkeh and the others in their pious community, the crucifixion is a symbol of millennia of repression, violence, and bloodshed against the Jews. Jesus on the cross represents not Christian salvation but persecution by Christians. For Asher to use his talent to paint a symbol so closely associated with those who have sought to eradicate Jews is an unpardonable sin.

Epigraph

An epigraph is a phrase or a quote that prefaces a book and foreshadows its themes. For this novel, Potok chose a quote by the artist Pablo Picasso: "Art is a lie which makes us realize the truth." Encountering this as the first sentence of the book tells the reader the book is about art and about the truth of art. The epigraph sets the stage for what is to come and cues the reader as to what to focus on. The book is not about Judaism, it is about art—the Orthodox community is just the setting in which the author examines the nature of art.

By keeping the epigraph in mind, the reader can zero in on what the author believes are the most important elements of the story. How is art a lie in *My Name Is Asher Lev*? What is the truth? Art is a lie in that it is merely a representation of something, not the thing itself. A painting of an apple is not an actual apple—that is, it is a lie. However, a painting of a ripe, juicy apple may convey the truth of how delicious a real apple can be. When this idea is applied to *My Name Is Asher Lev*, the reader may infer that Potok intends to show how Asher's actual paintings are not as important as the truth they reveals about his relationship to his family and community.

In this case, the source of the epigraph—Pablo Picasso—is relevant to the story. At the time in which the story takes place, Picasso was the most famous and successful living artist in the world. Asher's Uncle Yitzchok introduces his young nephew to the works of Picasso. Jacob Kahn had known and worked with him, and he instructs young Asher to spend one whole winter studying Picasso's masterpiece *Guernica*, a panoramic 1937 Cubist depiction of the horrors of the Spanish Civil War, before Jacob begins his apprenticeship. When Asher visits France, his first stop in Paris is Picasso's former studio in Montparnasse. Through his association with Kahn and his study of Picasso's work, Asher's ultimate work, the *Brooklyn Crucifixions* are inspired by Picasso's Cubist style, which allows him to portray Rivkeh's divided loyalties successfully, as she simultaneously looks toward her husband, her son, and up at the heavens in *Brooklyn Crucifixion II*.

Historical Context

Lubavitch Movement

The Chabad Lubavitch are a sect of the Hasidim on which Potok based the Ladover Jews in *My Name Is Asher Lev*. The global Lubavitch movement has been based in Crown Heights, Brooklyn, since around 1940 and is the largest mystical Orthodox sect of Judaism in the world today. Named for the eastern Russian town of Lyubavichi, not far from Poland, the sect was founded in the late 1700s by Shneur Zalman of Liadi.

Following a Nazi-led massacre of Jews in the early days of World War II, the movement's leader, Rebbe Yosef Yitzchok Schneersohn, relocated to New York City. In the years following the war, the movement expanded rapidly throughout many countries through the establishment of yeshivas in many major cities throughout the world. Lubavitchers study the Kabbalah, a mystical spiritual system that dates back to the thirteenth century and that focuses on the elusive nature of the relationship between the Master of the Universe (God) and those whom he created. Lubavitchers stress the importance of one's intellect over one's emotions and attach much significance to religious observations, holidays, traditions, rites, and rituals.

The Lubavitcher community is quite

structured. The Rebbe is the group's influential and revered spiritual leader. Followers define their closeness to the Master of the Universe in terms of their relationship with their Rebbe, and they trust him to make decisions that affect their lives. Such decisions include important things such as what to study in school, what career path to follow, and whom to marry. The followers believe that part of their soul resides within the Rebbe, and they can therefore trust him to know their strengths and weaknesses.

Lubavitchers adhere strongly to tradition, ritual, and Talmudic studies. Clothing and physical appearances are highly codified, diets are kosher, and many religious holidays and customs are practiced and celebrated regularly. The strict nature of these routines often keeps Lubavitchers away from mainstream culture and reinforces the insular, self-contained nature of the movement. Families are tightly knit, and children are expected to honor and obey their parents and other community elders. Unsanctioned behavior, such as Asher's flagrant pursuit of art, are highly frowned upon.

Joseph Stalin and the Gulag

Joseph Stalin (1878–1953) was the leader of the Soviet Union from the time of V. I. Lenin's death in 1924 until his own death in 1953. He instituted cruel policies and issued orders that resulted in the deaths of millions of people. His agricultural reforms resulted in a famine known as the Holodomor, in which millions of Ukrainians starved to death in 1932 and 1933 in retaliation for their opposition to Stalin's political policies. He sent millions of others—including a disproportionate number of Jews—to penal colonies in the Gulag, an inhospitable arctic region thousands of miles from civilization, where many died of starvation and exposure. Stalin's anti-Semitism (hatred of Jews) is well documented; in 1946, he stated that "every Jew is a potential spy" and called them, euphemistically, "rootless cosmopolitans," meaning disloyal to the state.

Compare & Contrast

- **1950s**: Crown Heights, Brooklyn, once an upper-class enclave for Manhattan's elite, is now a middle-class neighborhood of row houses with 75,000 Jewish residents, thirty-four major synagogues, and the headquarters of the Lubavitch movement. About 25 percent of the population is African American.

  1970s: During the July 1977 blackout, Crown Heights is hit especially hard by looters and arsonists, who turn the power grid failure into a "Night of Terror," according to the mayor. High poverty in the area prompts people to pillage and plunder a fourteen-block stretch of Brooklyn, including Crown Heights, in a riot that underscores the severity of socioeconomic and racial tension in the area.

Today: Following several decades of economic decline and racial violence, Crown Heights undergoes gentrification and continues to have thriving African American, West Indian, and Jewish communities. Ninety percent of the population is African American, and 9 percent is Jewish.

- **1950s**: The New York art scene is dominated by abstract expressionists, including Jackson Pollock, Willem de Kooning, Barnett Newman, and Mark Rothko, who live and work in Greenwich Village. Their often simplistic-looking, non representational works are championed by Leo Castelli, a Jewish-born Viennese art dealer whose eponymous galleries in New York led to the pop art movement of the 1960s. Pablo Picasso's *Garcon a la pipe*, painted in 1905, is sold for an astounding $30,000 to art collector John Hay Whitney.

1970s: Ileana Sonnabend, Leo Castelli's wife, opens the Sonnabend Gallery in Soho, establishing this lower-Manhattan neighborhood as a beacon of the international art scene, specializing in conceptual and minimal art.

Today: Jackson Pollock's *No. 5*, painted in 1948, is the most expensive painting ever sold at auction, commanding $140 million, when sold by Sotheby's in 2006 on behalf of media mogul David Geffen.

- **1950s**: The Lubavitch movement is based in Crown Heights, Brooklyn, and is led by the charismatic Rebbe Menachem Mendel Schneerson, a revered Jewish leader who is the seventh Chabad Rebbe.

  1970s: The Lubavitch world headquarters since the 1950s, 770 Eastern Parkway in Crown Heights, expands to serve a growing congregation and is considered a holy site by the Hasidim.

  Today: Still based in Crown Heights, the Lubavitch movement is no longer headed by a Rebbe; the Chabad belief is that the coming of the messiah is imminent, and therefore a leader for a new generation is not necessary.

- **1950s**: Provincetown, Massachusetts, formerly a whaling community in America's colonial era, is a summer resort area at the tip of Cape Cod popular with many writers and artists.

1970s: The Provincetown Business Guild is formed in 1978 to promote gay tourism.

Today: Provincetown is a gay mecca, and gentrification is further cementing its artistic heritage, with festivals staged year-round. Population remains steady at about 3,500 residents year round and 60,000 during the summer months.

The Night of the Murdered Poets alluded to in *My Name Is Asher Lev* was a real event in which fifteen Jewish writers were executed in a Moscow prison on August 12, 1952. Members of the group had been arrested in 1948 and 1949 and charged with espionage and treason, among other crimes, after having been jailed and beaten for three years. Five members of the group were active members of the Jewish Anti-Fascist Committee and had supported the Soviet war effort in World War II against the Germans. After the war, however, the Committee sought to rebuild the Jewish community within Russia and support Israeli statehood. Both goals were at odds with Stalin's vision for the Soviet Union in the cold war.

The Doctors' Plot, which also figures in *My*

Name Is Asher Lev, was another historical incident that further illustrated Stalin's anti-Semitic policies. Hundreds of physicians, most of them Jewish, were tried on trumped-up charges of plotting to kill Soviet officials. Many of those charged were killed outright, and others were sent to the Gulag. After Stalin's death in 1953, all charges were found to be baseless, and those who survived were set free. Thus, Stalin's death, as recounted in the opening of chapter 3, was a welcome relief for many Jews, especially those who had come from or still had family in the Soviet Union. Fear of recurring anti-Semitism was instrumental in the Lubavitcher movement to help relocate Russian Jews from the Soviet Union to Europe, the United States, or Israel throughout the 1950s.

Jacques Lipchitz

Potok has stated that he modeled Jacob Kahn on the Jewish artist Jacques Lipchitz (1891–1973), a Lithuanian sculptor who studied in Paris in the early twentieth century, where he was part of the "Esprit Nouveau" artists' community in the Paris neighborhoods of Montmartre and Montparnasse. His early work was Cubist in style, as he was influenced by the movement that was establishing itself in the area at the time, with his colleagues Pablo Picasso and Amedeo Modigliani, both artists whose work figures prominently in Asher Lev's artistic education. Lipchitz fled France at the outbreak of World War II and settled in Hastings-on-Hudson, New York, a sleepy suburb of

Manhattan. His career grew steadily after the war; he had several retrospectives at major museums around the country, and he once sculpted a Virgin Mary for the Catholic Church. From the 1960s until his death in 1972, he spent several months each year working in Italy.

Lipchitz and his family, though observant Jews, were not Hasidic, and for most of his life he remained ambivalent about Judaism, despite his marriage to an Orthodox Jew, Yulla Haberstadt. After a life-threatening illness when he was in his sixties, Lipchitz returned to the Lubavitcher sect and forged a relationship with the Rebbe.

Critical Overview

Coming on the heels of Potok's success with *The Chosen and The Promise, My Name Is Asher Lev* further cemented the author's reputation for deftly portraying the concerns of the American Orthodox Jewish community and the conflicting forces of religion and secular life. For Edward A. Abramson, author of the critical study *Chaim Potok*, the novel represents "a step forward in the subtlety and nuance of [Potok's] writing, having eliminated many of the flaws of his previous works."

Writing in the *Saturday Review*, Robert J. Milch commended the book as being "heartfelt and straightforward" and "narrated with a fluent simplicity that belies its intellectual depth and the technical skill of its construction." Guy Davenport, in a review for the *New York Times Book Review*, went further, praising it as nearly "a work of genius." David Stern, in a review for Commentary magazine, however, was less enthusiastic, saying that "as a portrait of the artist and a study of his growth and maturing, *Asher Lev* is without distinction." Anthony Barson, in a review for the *Christian Science Monitor*, agreed, calling Potok's conveyance of Asher's internship as an artist "dull, ponderous, [and] humorless." A contributor to the London *Times Literary Supplement* concurred that Potok did not convincingly convey Asher's artistic gift, but praised the book's "prayers, greetings, customs and attitudes of Hasidic Jews."

Several critics, noting the story's kunstlerroman format, compared *My Name Is Asher Lev* to James Joyce's *A Portrait of the Artist as a Young Man* (1916). As Potok wrote in a 1985 essay for *Studies in American Jewish Literature*, Joyce's novel "was almost as much a part of my growing up as were the Bible and Talmud." Both novels concern artists born into conservative cultures who find themselves on the outside of that culture looking in. For Stephen Dedalus in Joyce's novel, the culture is the oppressive Irish Catholic world of Dublin, where the boy, who desperately wants to be a writer, is expected to become a priest. Asher Lev, as the son of a highly respected aide to the Rebbe, is expected to assume a similarly respected position. Asher Lev's struggle to gain respect as an artist results in his exile from his Crown Heights community against his will. In Joyce's novel, Stephen voluntarily severs his relationship with his home and family. In addition to the works' thematic similarities, they have much in common stylistically as well. According to S. Lillian Kremer in an essay for *Studies in American Jewish Literature*, "Potok's experiments with interior monologue, stream of consciousness techniques and epiphany in addition to his fusion of socioreligious dynamic with individual character clearly reveal the substantive Joycean influence."

The novel's main theme, according to Warren R. True, writing in *Studies in American Jewish Literature*, is "the relationship of the artist to his culture." Importantly, True reinforces the notion that the book is not about Asher's rejection of

Judaism. Instead, the boy's conflict comes solely from the fact that "Judaism contains nothing in its literature or art to serve as a model for individual anguish and martyrdom despite centuries of recorded pain." The choice between art and Judaism is one that Asher would rather not make. He remains observant, even while he treads on thin ice with the Rebbe and his family. As Kremer states, "Unlike most of the characters in the writings of Bellow, Malamud, and Roth, who leave the religious life for the secular, those of Potok's novels bring the secular life into the religious."

What Do I Read Next?

- *A Portrait of the Artist as a Young Man* (1916) by James Joyce is a kunstlerroman, semi-autobiographical tale in which the hero, Stephen Dedalus, serves as a stand-in for the youthful Joyce.

Stephen longs to be a writer, but he finds this goal incompatible with his strict Roman Catholic upbringing in Ireland.

- *The Chosen* (1967) is Chaim Potok's first novel and tells of two Jewish boys growing up in Brooklyn in the 1940s. Reuven, a Modern Orthodox Jew, has a good relationship with his father. His best friend Danny is sheltered Hasidic Jew who has a troubled relationship with his father, who is grooming Danny for leadership within their strict Jewish community.

- *The Rebbe's Army: Inside the World of the Chabad-Lubavitch* (2005) by Sue Fishkoff examines the many young Lubavitcher couples called schlihim, who willingly relocate to towns big and small throughout the world to promote observant Judaism by establishing Chabad Houses, often on college campuses or in major cities.

- *Marc Chagall: What Colour Is Paradise* by Thomas David and Elisabeth Lemke (2000) is young-adult biography tracing the artist's youth in the Jewish neighborhood in Vitebsk, Russia. The book is heavily illustrated with Chagall's paintings, many of which are biographical, and with photographs. Chagall was deeply religious, and many of his paintings depict stories from the Torah.

- *Black, White & Jewish: Autobiography of a Shifting Self* (2002) by Rebecca Walker is the story of Walker's unusual life as the daughter of African American author Alice Walker and the Jewish lawyer Mel Leventhal. Finding herself at times ostracized in both the white and black worlds while being shuttled between her divorced parents—not to mention failing to fit in with her Jewish relatives—Walker relates her upbringing in locales as various as Mississippi, San Francisco, New York City, and Washington, DC.

- *Crown Heights: Blacks, Jews, and the 1991 Brooklyn Riot* (2006) by Edward S. Shapiro examines the repercussions of a 1991 incident in which a Hasidic motorcade driving through Crown Heights struck and killed an African American boy. Racial tensions in the multi-cultural neighborhood exploded with deadly consequences, highlighting the long-festering tensions between blacks and Jews here, with members of both groups believing themselves to be persecuted minorities.

- *Judaism: A Short Reader* (2010) by Dan Cohn-Sherbok and Lavinia Cohn-Sherbok is a beginner's guide to the history of the Jewish faith and introduces readers to Jew-ish beliefs and customs.

- *Wanderings: Chaim Potok's Story of the Jews* (1978) is a nonfiction illustrated history of the Jewish people over the past four thousand years, concentrating on how such a persecuted people has managed to survive in frequently inhospitable political and cultural conditions.

Sources

Abramson, Edward A., *Chaim Potok*, Twayne, 1986, pp. 58–81.

Barson, Anthony, "The Artist as a Novel," in *Christian Science Monitor*, June 14, 1972, p. 11.

Clarfield, A. Mark, "The Soviet 'Doctors' Plot—50 Years On," in *British Medical Journal*, Vol. 325, No. 7378, December 21, 2002, pp. 1487–89, http://www.ncbi.nlm.nih.gov/pmc/articles/PMC1390 (accessed May 31, 2011).

Davenport, Guy, "Collision with the Outside World," in *New York Times Book Review*, April 16, 1972, pp. 5, 18.

"Glossary—Key Jewish FAQ's," in *Chabad.org*, http://www.chabad.org/library/article_cdo/aid/10841 (accessed June 7, 2011).

Goldman, Peter, et al., "Heart of Darkness," in *Newsweek*, July 25, 1977, pp. 17–22, http://www.blackout.gmu.edu/archive/pdf/newsweek (accessed June 7, 2011).

"In the Goyish Mould," in *Times Literary Supplement* (London, England), No. 3683, October 6, 1972, p. 1184.

"Jewish Practice—Jewish Traditions and Mitzvah Observances," in *Chabad.org*, http://www.chabad.org/library/article_cdo/aid/32518 Practice.htm (accessed June 7, 2011).

Kremer, S. Lillian, "Dedalus in Brooklyn: Influences *of A Portrait of the Artist as a Young Man on My Name Is Asher Lev*," in *Studies in American Jewish Fiction*, No. 4, 1985, pp. 26–38.

Mahler, Jonathan, "Waiting for the Messiah of Eastern Parkway," in *New York Times*, September 21, 2003, http://www.nytimes.com/2003/09/21/magazine/waiti for-the-messiah-of-eastern-parkway.html (accessed June 6, 2011).

Milch, Robert J., Review of *My Name Is Asher Lev*, in *Saturday Review*, April 15, 1972, pp. 65–66.

"Night of the Murdered Poets," in *National Council on Soviet Jewry*, August 12, 2002, http://www.ncsj.org/AuxPages/081202MurderedPoe (accessed May 31, 2011).

Potok, Chaim, *My Name Is Asher Lev*, Knopf, 1972.

———, "The First Eighteen Years," in *Studies in American Jewish Literature*, No. 4, 1985, pp. 100–106.

"Provincetown Business Guild," in *Provincetown.com*, http://www.provincetown.com (accessed June 7, 2011).

Smith, Roberta, "Ileana Sonnabend, Art World Figure Dies at 92," in *New York Times*, October 24, 2007, http://www.nytimes.com/2007/10/24/arts/24sonnabe (accessed June 7, 2011).

Stern, David, "Two Worlds," in Commentary, October 1972, pp. 102, 104.

True, Warren R., "Potok and Joyce: The Artist and His Culture," in *Studies in American Jewish Literature*, No. 2, 1982, pp. 181–90.

Zaklikowski, David, "How Jacques Lipchitz Found G-d: The Rabbi and the Sculptor," in *Chabad.org*, http://www.chabad.org/therebbe/article_cdo/aid/393 Jacques-Lipchitz-Found-G-d.htm (accessed May 31, 2011).

Further Reading

Barkess, Joanna, "Painting the Sitra Achra: Culture Confrontation in Chaim Potok's Asher Lev Novels," in *Studies in American Jewish Literature*, No. 17, 1998, pp. 17–24.

> In this criticalessay, Barkessanalyzes *My Name Is Asher Lev* and *The Gift of Asher Lev* in terms of imagery and Freudian overtones in creating a schism, in which resides the concept of the Other Side.

Brent, Jonathan, and Vladimir Naumov, *Stalin's Last Crime: The Plot Against the Jewish Doctors, 1948–1953*, Harper Perennial, 2004.

> The authors trace Stalin's painstaking plans to create the appearance of a massive conspiracy of the Jews against the Soviet regime, which is discussed in *My Name Is Asher Lev* as the plot against the doctors. Brent and Naumov also discuss inconsistencies in the facts surrounding Stalin's death, indicating that his plot may have backfired on him.

Frankel, Ellen, *The Jewish Spirit: A Celebration in Stories and Art*, Stewart, Tabori & Chang, 1997.

> This book presents Jewish mystical

and folk tales from around the world, along with full color illustrations of Jewish artworks from museums worldwide.

Kouvar, Elaine M., "An Interview with Chaim Potok," in *Contemporary Literature*, Vol. 27, No. 3, Fall 1986, pp. 291–317.

Potok talks about the problems Jewish artists encounter with respect to religion, and particularly as they relate to Asher Lev.

Potok, Chaim, and Daniel Walden, eds., *Conversations with Chaim Potok*, University Press of Mississippi, 2001.

This collection of interviews between Potok and leading literature critics were conducted between 1976 and 1999. Potok discusses his own works, those of fellow Jewish writers, his literary influences, and how he prefers to see himself as an American writer who concentrates on a small slice of culture rather than as a Jewish writer.

Walden, Daniel, "Potok's Asher Lev: Orthodoxy and Art: The Core-to-Core Paradox," in *Studies in American Jewish Literature*, Vol. 29, 2010, p. 148.

Walden discusses the main conflict of *My Name Is Asher Lev*, namely "an observant Jew's confrontation with Western Art." He places the novel in its literary context with the works of Faulkner, Joyce, Flannery O'Connor, and other writers.

Suggested Search Terms

Judaism AND Chaim Potok

Jewish AND Chaim Potok

Orthodox AND Judaism

Hasidic AND Jewish

Joseph Stalin AND Jew

artist AND Chaim Potok

Brooklyn AND Chaim Potok

Lubavitch AND Chaim Potok

Chaim Potok

My Name Is Asher Lev AND Chaim Potok

bildungsroman

kunstlerroman